Well Beyond the Grace Period

Poems by Paul L. DeVore

ACKNOWLEDGMENTS.

The poem entitled "A Man Recently Young Moves Out" was published in Oberon, fall issue, 2014, under the title "Well Past the Grace Period: A Man Recently Young Moves Out".

The poem entitled "My Artichoke, Threw Caraway" was published in *Beloit Poetry Journal*; vol. 47, no. 1, 1996, under the title "It's a Plum Grape Fielding, but I Can Barley Till Rye."

The poems "Forgiving Father" and "Polly's Open Casket" were published in The Last Happy Chilhood. By Paul L. DeVore. 2011. barharbor-chalet@myfairpoint.net

FOREWORD TO WELL BEYOND THE GRACE PERIOD

I was blessed to have an older brother to bushwhack a trail both for life's early ascent and for the twilit stumbling down into wilderness. Over coffee and cards Irven spoke of the mice just beyond focus and of farces with hospital beds. He told me what he had concluded about manly playing of the final hands with chips dwindling. Here's the deal.

TABLE OF CONTENTS

◇◇◇◇◇◇◇◇◇◇◇◇◇◇◇◇◇◇◇◇◇◇◇◇◇◇

I.

WELL BEYOND THE GRACE PERIOD

◇◇◇◇◇◇◇◇◇◇◇◇◇◇◇◇◇◇◇◇◇◇◇◇◇◇◇◇◇

BORROWED TIME

When I arise to breakfast, I sense there's a fresh clock.
'Didn't apply for it. How am I so lucky?

Surely not from time given to others.
That account never held a saintly sum.

Maybe it's from lovers, who wouldn't notice.
Or those in misery; they wouldn't begrudge it.

'Isn't heralded by folks with capped teeth and cameras
.Perhaps everyone gives an unnoticed nano—many thanks!

HEAD WEAR

Over decades it led projects,
rolled because of some--
after which it was handed to me
on a platter, putatively silver.

Occasionally held high,
Sometimes hung down,
often hungover,
scratched, balding.

Early grown too big,
it was shrunk,
loose screws tightened,
and the whole screwed on again.

Hence, the wrinkles and bobbling.

DID I DRESS FUNNY AGAIN?

Picture a five-year-old who
won't wear sister's bonnet, trimmed in possum fur,
until the family convinces him he looks like wolfman.
So he wears it for his first day at school.

Skip ahead to a mawkish pinnacle:
squiring dates to coffee houses after concerts,
wagging tails and white tie--
rented splendor oddly fun.

Now the gala in the neighborhood.
Too cowardly to wear a mask,
I don tweeds, silk tie and
polished loafers with leather heels.

Before knocking, I stretch my arms
so that cuff links peep from the sleeves.
A jaunty tramp with painted-on mustache invites me in.
"Pretty sharp! Who are you supposed to be?"

GLAD RAGS

◇◇◇◇◇◇◇◇◇◇◇◇◇

Who am I fooling?
Not kids nor cameras:
sleeves all floppy, black dress shoes.
Yes, I heard the bouncer mutter "old fart."

Gravity is an imp on the stairs,
but a buddy here at the urinal.

For now, notch the belt.
Tuck for chrissakes your shirttail.
Twitch the no-ass trousers smooth.
Comb the comb-over and over.

Limp from the Men's into boozy air,
a lounge leopard wary of its prey.
Only...the party has moved on.
The grilles are clamoring down, the door locking.

HITCHHIKER

When my license and I were springy-young,
I imagined finding a comely wanderer
with hope in her face, talents in her pack,
the future surging inside her.

I'd swing wide the door, thought I,
grope for love, grab at secrets,
bend her to my will—or, likely,
be bent 'til death to hers.

Having driven and hitched
from wilds of taking to coves of giving
--sharing the journey with such as you--
devils no longer possess me.

They've fled to younger men
in helmets, headdresses, executive suites.
The manly willy, the feminine frilly
are faded into the rear view.

So make yourself comfortable
and remind me how life looks to a dreamer.
"How far do you want to go?"
bears no extra entendre.

BIKINIS IN LOW RESOLUTION

An old dog dreams in dawnsleep of romping again,
but the beach's glare teaches once more
that oiled-up twinklers desire the buck-hardy.

Better to corral praise-chirping grandcrickets,
name bagged gaggles of shells and flotsam,
skip proffered stones across wavelets.

The heart recalls brute wishes, curves deep in memory.
These trump feeble drives and failing eyes.

Play the grandfather cards deftly.
Perhaps a warmed goddess will grace us with a laugh.

WAVING A WAND

◇◇◇◇◇◇◇◇◇◇◇◇◇◇

Each has within grasp the power to conjure.
As I point my cane, observe!
A chair ten feet from me moves aside.
Cars stop; crowds part at my advance.

With a flourish I halt the headlong rush of children,
penetrate the fog of adolescence, soften hearts of jade.
Kindly burghers emblazon princely parking slots with my azure crest.
Curbs melt away; stairs meld into gentle ramps.
.

I met Liberation herself in an apron:
She held open the door to the Men's room.

Rappel as far as you can and then reach out.
Grab bars are civic love handles.
It pays richly to be handicapped;
'Can't recommend it enough.

FROWNS ALL THE WAY DOWN

Aslant to life all this week.
What is quiet about desperation?

Every bill, a hammer blow.
Rejections crack my bones.

Comfort food tastes ashen.
Reruns feel dated.

Pairs sum to five.
The language of intercourse is foreign, exhausting.

Families fix smiles and close ranks at my limping advance.
At night phones stay busy with one another.

For a body on hold there is only ulcerous peace.
None at all for a mind awake alone.

PANIC BUTTON

Many buttons; others yet to be invented:
One for those who've hit a glass ceiling and can't move up;
one to unpush when office lovers skate onto thin ice.

Young lovers sound alarms aplenty but crave more to push.

I sport mine as a large pendant
such as a doyenne might choose to make myopic girlfriends envious.

Forgetting the new gizmo (or disdaining it),
I napped amongst watered flowers until help happened.

Now it suits me, smells of me.
Facing thronging traffic from St. Ives, a simple test assures me I am not
alone;
a concerned voice asks whether I am okay.

And it comes with a lifetime guarantee.

THE KIDS EBB HOME

◇◇◇◇◇◇◇◇◇◇◇◇

Final shrieks, last potty, time check—OMG!

With quick, tight hugs and murmurs, they roll away, waving.

They leave hearts washed and minds reshaped,

teaching elders that fish make sauce and soys give milk.

Their sprouts race apace,

reaching for sun and filling corners.

Hugs from a baby stop time.

Stares from kindergartners are purgative.

We forget that tossing food is hilarious.

Dominoes are best with no rules.

B-bs are superior to bullets.

Blissful bubbles glisten, burst—and are replaced.

Mangled words draw praise.

Bitterness evaporates with a nap.

A kiss heals boo-boos and thundering.

How could Heaven compete?

AGING IN PLACES

When unriddling Kant and mastering Maya seemed urgent--
along with scaling an impregnable mate--
riding on a bus roof or being lost and found in the Sahara was abnormally
normal.

Nowadays I stipulate that guinea pig or creatures with many legs taste
good to locals.
I'm fine with creamed soup and chatty companions—thanks!
Tip: when you bite off too much, just chew slowly.

Hotels sail now, you know; you <u>can</u> take it with you.
View castles from the water--often their best side.
Each inch of map paves our nubbly knowledge.

Proper journeys meld minds
and end with brief weldings of cheeks and chests--
sweet rehearsals for the perfect farewell.

Bed welcomes you nightly--snug and rubbed, if you're lucky.
For now, keep stumbling through portals.
Read the poster: The aim of surviving is thriving.

CROSSROADS

A granddaughter enters a crisis center,
haunted by a bad draft of her first chapter of living.
Far away, the family's brash silverback
wheedles and bullies his way out of rehab.

She is too young to know possibilties, distrusts helping hearers,
pouts at signage.to the main way.
She is bewildered at being ditched,
not sure she wants to continue.

He is too wizened to sense death, dictates to those at his elbow--
editing footnotes now fading, outlining great projects, demanding
cigarettes.
Given directions, he turns the other way.
It worked wonderfully in the past.

If only they could talk, really talk, to one another!
But life is all an 'if only'--don'tcha think?
Now she's back on her roots, high on the vine--
bloomings and thorns yet to come

But the one who preached us into vastness--
telling the whys of life through orphaned chimps, unmated moths--
is flickered out and scattered.
How great he lived; how small we all die.

INVENTORYING THE STUFF

◇◇◇◇◇◇◇◇◇◇◇◇◇◇

Outnumbered by a house with three storeys,
we rattle about like seeds in a gourd,
accumulated stuff blocking my wheels.
Heat goes to places I'll never see again,
comforting spiders and squirrels.

Time to sit and sort, so that photos of us
smoking, skinny and smirking
don't join drop cloths and old shoes
in the dumpster.

Coveted items turn campy, at best,
losing the power to wow or woo--
as the will to do either rusted::
cigarette case, size 12 opera pumps.

We save baby pictures, of course--
no longer scanning faces for promise.
We know the endings of these start-ups.

Some stuff that is headed out deserves a final look:
a scratched 45 of "Shake, Rattle and Roll"--
how meanings do shift!

A letter from an old carton crackles at the creases.
It arrived generations ago to a boy who learned
'quest' and 'jubilant' in penmanship more elegant
than his family's. Auntie wishing me a happy birthday.

The rest are cards:
gussied-up glossies of monuments,
rhymes that could line a highway,
cards wishing you merriness in wartime.

You wonder how hucksters
persuaded us to squeeze unnuanced emotions into a few
that fit racks neatly—each card offering
space only to write the expected cliché.

Artful displays of glittering cards
(some from banks or car dealers)
make hostesses heady,
visitors, envious. Blood sport.

Cheer is the common denominator.
'Happy' despite infidelities and poverty?
'Congratulations' on your dead-end job,
pointless degree, unwanted child?

Is this the very best we can send?
I pocket the letter from Auntie
and leave the rest to be recycled--
again and again.

A MAN RECENTLY YOUNG MOVES OUT

Everything is out of the closet now.

From overhead, a clutch of caps
fouled meaty by man suet.
Fingerprints tell of dusty homers and sawn wood,
of tugged-down hunkerings with gun and camera.

Here's poker chips and cards enough
to parry with a dozen liars.
But boxed-up now, gone the way of
dominoes, checkers, cider, uncles.

Framed portraits of Mom, Dad, the kids
all face the wall like bad boys.
A proud family but broken,
liable to fade in bright sun.

Neckties pretty as panties, dated as magazines.
When did I wear wide paisleys?
Briefly they made the man,
turned a raw kid into live bait.

From a Rolodex, cards spill out.
Two addresses for one name, the change undated.
Names of babies now married and balding again.
Defunct emails for the living; phone numbers for the dead.

Everything quick and boy-careless:
A social roster with no zip or area.

A drawer jammed with nesting materials:
scraps of wrap from our first Christmas.
Postcards and photos of no clear value--
Just impossible to replace.

Passports for a man with a beard still dark.
Gold coins that don't buy bread; they just gleam.
At the back of the drawer a condom,
the foil too wished-over and wallet-warped to read.

Beneath everything a living will and a final testament await their turns.

The sense of demise is not wrong.
These pack rats are long-since gone:
Young fiddler and athlete who wouldn't play ball;
the swashbuckler I never quite was;
a Dad worrying along for decades;
lecturer, manager, merchant, son--
an all-American crowd leaving me to sift what they've done.

How curious to review the they that is me!
With such false starts and sudden turns,
what hope that an old junker can make it around the block?
At least, as I lift a stack of drawers,
I can choose the music for this passing.

A HOME IS NOT A HOUSE

Please do raise the shade, but do not ask again: "How are we feeling?"
One of us is achy-old and given to falling; that did not change overnight.
Nor do days change: I count pills, catalog ironies,
cobble together cross words and puzzles.

I've grown adept at toenail Zen and hopper meditation....
do you want to hear all this?

The sun room runs on reruns and amateur footage.
Now on the screen: vacation videos of churches, faces and beaches.
At the tables: mossy tales with trite morals, hoary jokes.
After coffee I wade into a torrent of images and words,
pecking out wisdom giblets to forward to folks
to whom this matters; although they neglect to say so.

Fusillades of flatware cut the fog.
Reports of plate upon plate warn that lunch has thawed.

When we owned and were owned,
we were silken rugs, smoothened whiskey, redolent reds.
Our carved bed was wide, with a vista to the mainland.
We crossed continents, collected marquetry and ikat,
lost contact, palavered and survived--with films to prove it.
Journals and negatives and positives
are cramped in with images and letters of forebears
in a box under my narrow bed--a capsule open to receive my times.

A few intimates, most alive, crowd the night stand
as though awaiting chairs.

We planned and planted, razed and built.
Here I do not bang nor pry nor screw anything.
Toggles fetch light or sound--never cutting or shaping.
No whirring or whining, risk or joy.

Outdoors I prune and gather to good effect,
but the bushes lack essential beauty: I did not plant them.

A brisk vestal pops in with a couple of ha-ha-has --
to which a loving striper adds magazines and tra-la-las.
My shift here never ho-ho deepens,
but at home surely they talk breasts and balls.

To vestals you are unfailing, whatever you spew.
In this sanctuary it is forgiven to piss in your pew.

They are loving sisters, not mothers--never lovers.
What is my best line? "Please, wipe my chin again!"
They wash me daily, but only down to there.
Once, soaping together was a slow art.
Now the naughty box is locked and sealed seemly.

They mean well. We all do. Meaning to be mean is cast out.
Shriek out curses, bite hard twice...your brain is washed.

A ride is not a car.
The van runs from here to there--
no swings to the curb to chat with neighbors,
flirt with ex-wife, first love...whoever is alive out there.
"Driver, just hang a left, pass GO,
breeze through the countryside--blow air through our hair!"
"So, you'd like to visit the mountains? the sea?
We'll see if enough others sign up."

There is a curtain between us now.
My hands are mitts that touch but do not feel.
You know this.
I hug your living body in order to stand,
But I cannot animate it or detain you for long.
I accept that.

This is not your first last look--only the latest.
Perhaps _I_ am having a last look.
You never know.
Certainly, I do not know.

Do the kids keep in touch?
Do they, really?

Passion, crafting, gestures at the world
dwindle to protocols, immutable and safe.
I cloak myself in meals, pills, visits.
I've already said this, I think.
I draw these around me and lay me down.

Memories, barely sensed, scurry into the tangles--
Faces scarcely glimpsed.

Was I very unkind just now,
or is that yesterday...tomorrow?
Tell me: How can I know that I am good if I must always act nice?
Why did I come here, remain here...why?

Are these childish questions? Am I childish?
Just tell me: Should I grant you power of eternity?

CAFETERIA CLATTER

◇◇◇◇◇◇◇◇◇◇◇◇◇◇

We arrive with shuffling feats of walkership
to jovial scrums over seating—
cracking jokes and sopping yolks.
Debates over prunes begin again.

I see Elena deploying frayed snapshots
of strapping grands and toddling greats,
ready to duke it out for looks and brains
with anyone who sits opposite.

Nearer, I hear widows just back from rehab
oozing news of pills, procedures, new parts--
lexicons bursting like sunburnt figs.
Each just happens to have the world's best surgeon.
Dropped names mar the floor.

Gents at my table recount heroic deeds
among financial minefields: "I'm still here to tell about it!"
Little did I suspect that unexploded ordnance lodges
in every bank and brokerage.
I learn that my condo isn't in the top 100,
that my RV is not nearly as large as Chuck's.

Isn't that the way with chats?

During wheres and hows, froms and nows,

wraiths drift from the eyes to flick the aura.

Your crowd sizes up the gang across the table.

By daily miracles few hit an off-ramp with no return.

No records or bones are broken.

Another day of breathing deeply and fumbling medications—usually

recovered.

Aides set the schedule for visits, excursions, naps.

For some, breakfast leads to pastimes;

for others, to contemplation of times past.

I have letters to compose, ear worms to conduct: business enough.

Could be worse; hopefully not.

Could be better; probably not.

It's just life, you know.

A MIGHTY-WHITE SAC SPILLS OVER

Must have been smuggled whiskey;
certainly not our Christmas cider.
The taciturn Jack opens a rotting mucksack
that explains his many troubles.

First out are crumpled slogans--almost to laugh at.
He hurls a hail of daggers sharpened to monosyllables:
wops, kikes, fags—dissing half the species as cunts.
Ever the veteran, he digs out slope, slant...back to kraut and jap.

They wheel him away as the blames grow:
lazy kids, welfare queens, aliens.
I glance into the bag and see more hiding in the wordpile.
"But you do like WASPs?" I shout.
"What the hell do they have to with it?!"

PLAY PERIOD: HAVE I REALLY BEEN WORKING ON THE RAILROAD?

Sisters in the same class,

one teasing, the older sassing sweetly back.

Greetings and chatter crescendo

until teacher says to take off shoes and begin.

"Sit straight, and count so I can hear you!"

Floyd closes his eyes and embroiders the moves.

No one corrects him; no need.

Teacher says: "Put your shoes on and find a partner!"

Girls mince through simple dance steps nimbly.

Boys show little promise, peppering us with jokes.

Teacher waits for boys to stop showing-off.

Girls are unimpressed. That's how it is.

The helper leads our marching song.

"Lift your knees; everyone sing!"

Dan plays air banjo as we stomp.

Young, I played along wonderfully with recorded concertos,
but when playing alone: ghastly rasping in playback.
I sang beside monotones who supposed they navigated intrIcacies
that we others were singing.
Across the circle I see Cal mouthing the marching song.
Is he singing outside his head?
Certainly, he isn't marching.
Was I?

It ends as it began: imagined gusto
as I contentedly float along.
I swell with urgent purpose, know what needs doing,
but realize that I accomplish little.

More songs--with flights of harmony:
"Down by the Old Mill Stream";
"Let me Call You 'Sweetheart'":
"Roll out the Barrel!"

Teacher and helper pass out cookies
amidst thanks and goodbyes.
We board the bus to the retirement home,
wondering aloud what awaits us for lunch.

PLAYED-OUT

Jozef always deals and narrates:
"Eighter from Decatur—too bad.
"Pair of bullets, treetops tall! Everybody folding?"
He rakes in the worn cards and shuffles.

He deals for hours every day, slapping down the deck for a break.
"'Back soon. 'Better leave my chips alone!"
His hand sweeps above a barren tabletop.

His wife explains: "'Lovely bunch of guys.
"They were all in steel together . . . and rails.
"'Lots of friends at the funerals.'"

Refreshed, Jozef pauses before dishing out cards.
"Any chance the merger will work? How could it?"
He cranes to look beyond me.
"Can we get another deck? This one's killing me!"

I hand him the old deck from the next table,
watch as he deals to the vacant chairs.
I ease into the one next to him, reaching for cards.
He sizes me up, looks away.
"That's just a bonepile; leave it be!"

RECALLING AWFULLY LATE

◇◇◇◇◇◇◇◇◇◇◇◇◇◇

"Fine! And how've <u>you</u> been?"
Off-the-shelf, generic cheer
oozes down my face as the widow stares—
embers graying to ash.

I manage to blurt her name,
stammer our history in the chill.
Unfertilized egoshells crack easily.
Ever after that she is bluntly humpty.

BRUSHING OBLIVION

Not the flashing, wailing code red--
hot, public and helpered.

It's a frigid chain ratcheting crudely
through fraying bundles of meaning.

The shell of daily who and why
is cracked.

Life is an unruly meeting; or is it a party
    or a sacrament?
You cannot say.

Wastrels feel this oftener, we suppose;
but popes too get icy touchings.

They seek deliverance and wisdom.
I settle for the veneer of bluster.

You'll drift beyond charts and protocols.
I cannot help you—save by taking away the surprise.

Don't dwell on it.
The void offers no dividend.

Tack into smells of coffee and bacon.
Sail to a sunnier day and drop anchor.

LIGHT VISIONS

Time was, we shuffled through earthly toils--heads down, chins up--
believing that when our earthly slog ended,
parting curtains would dazzle us with splendor--world without end!

We saw it on card racks, mailed friends the proof:
squadrons of valedictorians, virginal and fecund,
in sensible sandals and loose swaddling,
with brushed tresses and wings,
meeting in headlong flight to sing to uncertain shepherds
sleeping with their sheep by night--

That light, with trumpets, banners and rays
embossed with half the gold of Christendom,
expanding to pilot the Magi, gathered in soft circlets over sacred heads
to illumine believers' hearts, reanimate the dead. Amen!

Over centuries divine radiance faded into the
glowing punch bowls of weddings
and gaudy twinkles of Santaland,
Sunlight became UV to be blocked at spring break.
Fireworks awe kiddies--
joys with no mystery.

To be sure, cardinals of science in ivory offices write

of miraculous sightings that laymen must take on faith:

stars dying and reborn, nebulae unfathomably far

and ungovernable devils with black power beyond the imaginings of prophets--

joyless mysteries.

Yet a new effulgence is reported by gowned, gaunt seers arising from gurneys:

an exit light in the velvety cavern of dying.

What could this enigma signify?

Pulp films tell of luminous fetal wights, terrible or wise--

with a genius for selling tabloids at checkout lines.

Myself, I suppose that it is a trick of legerdebrain sparking mightily to reboot,

much like the setting sun flaring as it sinks into the ocean.

ROSEBUDS IN WINTER

Time to rewrite the scene; can't have Lothario flopping athwart.
Volunteers will do the hard work and heavy breathing, twisting at
mirrors.
We've done the cells' bidding long enough.
Now we enjoy love without infinite hopes or fears.

You are no longer inhibited by babies flitting in the dark;
though a graying daughter watches with starchy documents in hand.
So you move in public with oblique signals, never touching by accident.
I know that you pinch my cheek back not to show my teeth
but to see if I will accept, unblinking, a smear of desire.

Even with shades open, macular mystery sets a mood.
Feet, ears are not just entry points, but snuffling destinations.
Your little back is a soft canvas that I paint over and again
until every fiber is stroked, every nerve tinted--
reaching then to strum a sarabande from the ribs.

Fondling and foolery, dawdling and fiddling
still have their turns,
Spooning a cool haunch becomes an end in itself--
not just a beachhead for invading the booby-trapped front.

Flannel is comfier than silk; rounded chuckles supplant sharp gasps.

Prolonged gurgles bring giggling accusations.

Posing like a movie moll, you proclaim:

"I'll give you one hour to stop all this before I call the cops!"

Palming an exposed shoulder, knuckle-nuzzling hollows or lying cheeks to cheeks,

We tease about bits that confound x-rays, slow cremation.

"I was a great beauty, you know?"

"Even better now" says I, dozing off.

Our past lives have become all foreplay.

Joined magnets needn't consider who made the first move.

GRAMPY'S FREE SPEECH

◇◇◇◇◇◇◇◇◇◇◇◇◇◇

Legs gone, only words gambol now.

Tumble the dice and call out imaginary numbers.

Simplify the real, engorge the fancy.

Unfreighted by guilt or forgiveness,

guileless by association,

commands become caring:

"Always choose kindness—starting now!"

Curses soften to melody, as singing out. . .

"Bilious cheese-paring smell-fungus!"

SMELLING LILACS IN RECOVERY

Mollycoddled among pillows, I see 10 become 11, then the noontime
horn.
A dear, dear supplicant with clattering tray holds forth tidbits, cajoles.
But nothing is so tempting as another nap.

They manage my pain, banish newscasts.
Only as a dream do I recall slamming a snooze alarm or batting a ball.
Procrastination is mine. Why leave the dessert bar?

They laugh and point because I start smiling.
I chuckle because a technician says I'm type A--
clearly confusing me with Dad, who died young.

The young man above me speaking brightly,
waving a searching little light,
has so much of life still to pass through.

He wants me to focus hard on an aquamarine I.V. drip.
Instead, I dive fearlessly from a glider into a submarine.
Now I shoo marauding turkeys from a market hall by Gaudi.

Sleeping further can't be bad.
Being born to mother was shocking, I'm told.
But being borne through this is not.

UNSEEMLY FACEOFFS

The finest families do it:
toss something amongst heirs,
and there is furious slapping.

I'd sooner melt a ring,
smithereen a platter,
launch paintings on the tide...

Rather comfort strangers
with quilts and rugs
than trip up caring kin.
Things pose as the stuff of life.
We cherish some, use them for a bit--
then pass them along, burnished or tarnished.

Learn from the centurions at Golgotha:
share wine, wit and cheese;
trust fate's dice to divide trophies.

LIFE IN THE GREAT HERETOFORE

All set out from Eden down a wondrous slope
that we will not ascend later.
Joy is not locked in a hereafter
but granted freely at the outset.

True, there is no easy bliss, late or early.
I cannot speak of the time before I was me:
when I was one with mother and her breasts.
But I know there were pinpricks and burps--
and the desolation of weaning.

I see me toddling around playgrounds,
excited by exotic others.
I pump swings to see beyond treetops,
at bliss with the cosmos until dark and dinner--
hating to take time to eat or sleep.

Rain falls, toys break, pets die.
After the popcorn and derring-do,
house lights go up and you walk home.
Does this cancel joy or frame it?
You know the answer; I do anyhow:
living is a two-step of infinite choruses.

Finished with leaning forward,
I look back at my trail across the workaday plain.
Everywhere I see glitterings in the mud--
some of restless hormonal magma beneath,
most of happy coinage washed bright by the mind.

Think of tender touches, reaching shelter in a storm.
Remember joking, weeping, singing with others,
beginnings and completions, hearty accolades, gentle consoling.
It takes a lifetime to tally the pleasures of a lifetime.

Do not bank on visions of steady heavens beyond ken.
These have high walls, badlands of derision, moats of blood.
Curses on excluders, the brutest animals.
We see dogs buddy with lions or nurse piglets.
Blessed are beings that share.

I saw a world saved from war and wept as it turned to warring for peace.
We poured the riches of a new land into carburetors and doodads.
I had the unfathomable luck to have a light skin that kept me bobbing
atop the eddies.
My fondest wish is that those with harder roads reach contented peace.

Events collide, but there is no grand collusion to life--
nor injustice in death.
Neither visionaries nor dictators persist.
However, there is a thrust beyond the individual.

Tricked-out in beards or breasts, our species is god of the universe.
Despite infinite divagations into dry sand, our muddy mainstream
breaches dams of bullion, topples carapaces of stone.
And we are privileged to ponder the riddles of existence.

Hopes and guilt from my own potential are moot.
I was that I was and am ready to make way.
'Just want another look around before the light goes dim..
Besides, I see coffee and dessert on the table.

ANYONE EVER LIVE HERE?

◇◇◇◇◇◇◇◇◇◇◇◇◇◇

It's where I receive bills and return calls,
but it's merely a model home.
Push that unwired doorbell a dozen times
and freeze to death waiting.

Fine wines in the rack are dusty,
Cheery birch in the fireplace was never lighted.
I've strewn collectibles around to make the place seem lived-in,
hung the walls with degrees, left poems out to view.

But there are unfinished projects in the closet
and a cellar full of things beyond repair.
Really, with no guests dropping crumbs or shedding hair,
home's a misnomer, isn't it?

Frankly, development was not carried very far.
Party Lane never connected to my driveway.
Legacy Boulevard remains a broad stripe on the plat.
Lonely, yes—and peaceful. Thanks for stopping by.

II.

TAKING IT OR LEAVING

◇◇◇◇◇◇◇◇◇◇◇◇◇◇◇◇◇◇◇◇◇◇◇◇◇◇◇◇◇◇◇◇◇

NEW BROOM

We dropped off a bag of dresses, still presentable.

"About time!" says I.

Seeing that I was presentable,

She left me too.

SPARKING

Struck a match, then thought to drop it cold:
Phone number scribbled on an envelope.
Handclasp, polite; cup of decaf, dreadful.
Kiss too cool to raise insurance rates.

Smart money said this would flame out.
Then an exchange of photos--
hostage visages sent innocent;
though with bulging holsters.

At night the portraits glowed, searing papers.
Poems, letters smoked between the lines.
Detectors sensed nothing.
No one knew to drag in hoses, counselors.

LOVING BUT LEAVING

Loving we are, but desire wanders away
to whimper at crouching shadows.
Despite soft touches at night,
lunch at hard noon is a face-off.

In our orbit books lose meaning.
Food has no savor.
Grievances flash and thunder.
The house cannot be saved.

A professional shoveler buries the past.
Another rakes the estate.
What now? Get religion?
Play the field?... or just lie in it awhile?

She lives solidly at sea level,
respects the ebb and flow,
grazes resources lightly,
walks firm and talks real.

I'll fashion another tower,
share the balcony with a lady
thrust-breasted with pride.
We shall prefer beauty to news.

Or I'll perfect this alone
and preserve it with alcohol.
Why, in middle age, must I grow up?
Is there wisdom beyond habits?

A MAN'S HOME

Gothic dorms fool only proctors.
Apartments lack swards.

Condos grow ghosts,
and the paint is wrong.

I found my castle,
but it was not your home.

Did you feel locked in?
This is clearly key.

As you leave
I know you'll kill the lights.

HOW DARE WE?

Counselors assume the worst.
Lawyers stipulate as much.
Hostesses and kids
mull the quandary: just how bad is it?

Townsfolk debit a tidy sum,
compound it, and distribute shares:
"The way I heard it...."
"It must have started...."

Best friends, best-meaning,
resort to bromides and forceps:
"Let it all out!" "Get it out!"
"Silence is the greatest rage of all."

That we share still a soft fondness
seems an undetonated opportunity,
a flaw in the script,
an unclean break awaiting cautery.

Yo! If you fancy angry divorces, look to those that bolt from the blue
with Mercury, in dacron, serving the papers.
For color, find a channel where hubby phones from a motel bed
or the little woman brings a moving van to the house.

Why wait for divorce to celebrate rage?

Think of unions begun struggling in a car,

anniversaries marked by smashing plates,

marriages propped-up so that kids can be beaten by a familiar hand.

The menu of anger is varied enough for all palates.

It does not need us as catch of the day.

MISSING PERSON

This is not my woman;
though I see the resemblance:
lobes and breasts familiar,
but they do not throng the mind.

Mine aged none in twenty years;
this fake shriveled at a glance.
We've jinxed the mirrors;
neither of us looks good.

My helpmate touched me knowingly,
suffered me gladly.
This housemate friend
sees only a fool.

HALF ALONE

Separation is a three-day holiday.
Buy the mink dildo, the Harley.
Pick up dancers in leg-warmers,
their breasts tattooed.

Then old newspapers take stage-center.
It's unthawed meals, unsplit bills.
Kicking and tossing,
scratching and snacking as pastimes.

The fridge goes whorehouse:
beer, pickles, shriveled lemon.
Larder is grad school:
tuna, soup, chips, wine.

Dust lolls under and atop.
All legs seem uneven.
The shrieking teakettle amused us.
What were we thinking?

In sleep, a velvet finger grazes me.
I catch the moth, clutch it fluttering, crush it weeping.
I have been too long a half
to become whole alone.

COMING APART

Another woman has fallen apart.
I did not drop this one; my hands were good to be in.
She preferred a shelf beyond easy reach, involving teetering risks.

Was it too hot up there, too just right?
Did I squeeze too hard, as boys test snails?
'Watch too loosely as she fledged at the verge?

Even better hands won't soon restore her.
There are parts missing:
swept away or never formed.

A frivolous accusation:
at certain moons and musics I became--
a vampire, a tiny borer who ate so much
that she collapsed inward.

I chew her up; she now spits me out.
Your Honor perceives that this lacks
prima facie bona fides
(And other manly passwords).

I'm okay; thanks for asking.
Macho American steel:
old hitches and squeaks,
new dents and rattles.

Someday soon I'll flunk inspection,
a junker no longer polluting.
I'll sputterbang towards sunset--or just
around the bend, if hailed intently

IT CAN'T BE JUST ME

Everyone is crabby as all Hell!

Receptionists answer sweetly but never understand what I need.

I say "Fuck 'em!" "Fuck you!" I yell.

'Can't all be menstrual; 'can't all be old wives.

The guys don't drink as much coffee nor sleep as badly as I do,

so what is their problem?!

It's a breakdown of civility, something in the air.

Hey! You know what I mean!

Do I have to spell it out?!

DISSOLUTION

She fears that I'll drop down, frothing and brief.
But the dying is piecemeal slow.
Weeds run to seed.
The razor knicks blood.

Out of bed without desiring it;
back to bed without desire.
I neither plan nor record.
Was it sunny today?

Too sober to drink, too tired to sleep,
I discover the measure of it:
when a man stops feeding pets
he is wasting utterly.

RIDDLED FAMILY

Second mortgage, plus or minus,
a function of first wife, if-and-only-if
all subsets of in-laws are divided by ex's.
Hard to find the software; no answers in back of book.

She once said: "I love you because
"you are the father of my children"--
gently mimicking their mother.
Mocking the truth, but gaily.

So help me solve issue number one
for a marriage without issue:
the emotional half-life of step-lives
pushed and pulled rudely...any remainder?

Kids are us!
Heads down, in the swim,
how many Moms can they fit in?

For a generation that barely hangs,
marriage ghosts quickly crowd the guest room.
Old wife, second wife, new wife--
"Get a life!"

Will Oedipus solve this one?

This one does not know.

This Oedipus knows very little.

TURNING POINTS, PUNCHLINE

Spitting image, bundle of prodigy.
Blow out candles, wishing.
Write Santa, confident.
Tooth Fairy as real as quarters.

First bike with training wheels;
you never forget how.
First breast in training bra;
you never forget.

Car, prom, college, wife: hurrying into living.
At anniversaries you're the straight man.
Be straight! Be a man! Get the gag?

Now my dear permitted teat, my licensed lap
has opted to ex herself out.
Is that an absolute scream or what?!

Hey! If you can't take it,
'might as well tell the paper
to print now your punchline
among the others who died today.

III.

FAMILY MATTERS ABSOLUTELY

POLLY'S OPEN CASKET

For the lithe blue-blood who became a helpmeet in the Dust Bowl,
hanging laundry and corralling kids in the spray from oil wells,
the syringes and glass straws give way to stunned pomp and long-stemmed
lilies.

The congregation is competent at living but amateur at death,
Fumbling out rehearsed clichés.

Liars! Cowards!
Can you not speak death, or do you disgrace age by not knowing?

Polly is not sleeping; she is dead like a dog awful beside the road.
She will not rise up to be my mother now here, nor ever anywhere.
She will slump away like a baby bird fallen to the tidying of ants.

They mean well. They bring goodness. Their handshakes are cups of
warmth.
Abrupt babies are shushed into reverence.
Folks shuffle past the casket, catching shoes in the carpet.
This is the embrace they offer.

Those who wait outside, smoking, to manage traffic or move dirt –
I salute you. It is a hard living.
You who drained blood, washed hair, stuffed cheeks
and daubed them with color;
you who left the breasts intact by calculation, the womb by coincidence –
you were her devoted last admirers.

As for young sir who accepts an untaxed tip for preaching that her pains
fit a plan,
her early death accomplished an unknown good –
let him consider well his own mother or wife before repeating the script.

There is mystery enough without fogging by rote.

The memorial for a mere good mother?
Forty years later a cousin widens her eyes:
"There is something you just did that was just like Polly.
"Don't ask me what, but it was Polly."

FORGIVING FATHER

Much to forgive a big old farm boy for God:
His sneezes made the house jump.
Bedsprings sang to his snoring.
He grinned as farts ambushed the family.

He was called to travel the wide country, hitching and hopping,
sweeping floors to sleep on, picking fruit to eat.
Preaching sweaty, Dad trumpeted the steely courage of David,
whispered with shining eyes of fallen sparrows in the eye of God.

Much to be forgiven:
Shins that grew shiny.
Hair suddenly yellow.
Was that nice to spring on us?

Dad buried the dead and married the afflicted.
He also played at farming, sweating clean through his belt.
Desk-soft, Dad cut fence posts in the sun, and they brought him down.
He turned back to the earth, and it welcomed him in.

IV.

UP THE DANUBE

BUCHAREST INVADED BY AMERICANS

After museums and churches and squares
we flee the bus a final time near the crumbling dungeons of Vlad the
Impaler,
passing before Dracula's weather-withering bronze gaze.

Wheeled walkers crawl across a moat of cobblestones to lunch at Caru Cu
    Bere.
The high-ceilinged sanctum of stained glass was never a cathedral—not a
    holy place.
Gilded arches and painted alcoves were tarred amber by smokers of the
    Belle Epoque sybarites, aristocrats and sycophants.
Bones in the vaulted kitchens beneath are freighted with braised viands to
    be consumed with bubbly chrism.

Afterwards, we confront prune dumplings, grouped in threes and looking like the bald testes of a monster.

"Helluva note, serving prunes to geezers!"
A tanned princess, drooping with jewelry, sniffs: "Plums! They were plums!"

"Did anyone take a photo of me with Badass Vlad?"

LOVE IN BELGRADE

In the fortress park, folks nod, offer me help.

They joke, jog, interrupt dog fights.

Honking car horns jar us—but no one dies.

Olga arrives on canes to offer a banknote of 500 billion "For just pennies
on the dinar!"

Toothless, she laughs at the joke she has learned to repeat.

As I pay five dollars for the freakish note, she blurts "I love you!"

Bemused by the overstatement, I pat her arm: "I love you too, Olga."

"Is good. I love you, and I very much like dollars!"

QUESTING FOR AFFORDABLE GRAILS

◇◇◇◇◇◇◇◇◇◇◇◇◇

The visions change and remain out of focus.
We purchase a beauty, but the search—for what?--begins again,
driving us up the next hill and down the street.

Armed with magical slivers of silver, of gold, of platinum,
we hunger for something in good taste...or good-tasting,
authentic...or said to be so.

Burdened by cadres of recipients at home,
we hope to return with things that embody what we've seen--
and do so in ways that maintain their surprise untarnished.

We were promised experiences to cherish and now seek emblems--
photographed in perfect light or
crafted with skills and imagination that surpass our own.

That's what dollars are for.

We feel like diligent, selfless crusaders.
To merchants we are fish seeking hooks.

Overheard: "It's so hard. They never like the gifts I bring home."

V.

SPENT YOUTH

◇◇◇◇◇◇◇◇◇◇◇◇◇◇◇◇◇◇◇◇◇◇◇◇◇◇◇◇◇

MY ARTICHOKE, THREW CARAWAY

Since my heroin--mint in the berry hyacinths--in our greener salad days
Never hemped nor hedged in her melon voice nor pawpawed my clumsy ways,
I now mince no worts--cauliflower a flower--and sencereally wish to show her
Why I tractor alfalfa world around and on what grounds sow clover.

I think it was parsley poppy-clove for this gal who pepsin chives.
Myrrh I'vy cedar, my soul nosegay; but when she's gone . . . endives.
Young poppies like to spearmint and waste much thyme on cinnament
(All despice the voice of resin, which pines fir passion's fruit in its season)
But thistle never nettle more; she's reached marjoram, mustard score!
And now the laurel leaf at bay her berry herbbane wish to play.

She sesame, at last: "I cantaloupe but marijuana."
My artichoke, threw caraway, and dreamed a savory drama!

I garlic dared--if truth be told, the mere hope made me pallid--

To toss and savor, dress, undress, this fit-for-Caesar salad.

Hence: "Lettuce, when the nightshade's down" (Bold! As though I'd known herbivore!)

"Disport ourselves from root to crown dill harvests yield no more."

Ah, soon we'edtumbled well, for lentil did she know

How mocha in me this seedling wish had long begun to grow.

For of all the tempting cinnsamen, this rose-hipped, mallow bud

Does stir a fiery sap in me . . . . "Oh, be my constant cud!"

(And who but herbicides?)

WORD SLUT

Talk about needing the words!
Sang froid makes her flush hotly.
Just ask her to bathe after a night of talk;
she fears that you'll doze on the wordy spot.

Sweetie shoplifts invaluable vowels.
Commas leak through her bra;
thighs all knicked by x's,
sometimes y's.

Oddments of Mandarin in the freezer,
neologisms half-baked.
We skitter across dropped nouns
and lopped participles.

Watch yourself!
I am inflamed fit-to-bust
spontaneously into
perfervid conflagration!

CAP GUYS

You see them at the pump, gassing trucks
loaded with gear, brush, deer.

At the dump, they heave bags, construction debris--
clapping shoulders and palavering.

With hard hats on, wielding saws or shovels,
the cap is nearby or, anyhow, implied.

Folks give me caps that reek of golf or sailing.
These don't count; they count me out.

I slip bare-headed by, wearing rings--
too pallid to merit a fraternal cap...although

No one minds that my hands and tires are soft
when it's time to deal cards.

SORTING LENTILS

The package warned to sort them, so sort I did--
laboriously pinching black ones out,
curious hot-orange ones that looked wet off a beach,
and a few speckled ones--
before I began to doubt.

I fingered those that were wrinkled or thin or bent in upon themselves
and threw them out too,
plus a very few that had sprouted early.

At last, out dropped a stick and a stone, lying large across the lentil cobbles.

Out they went,
along with a lone albino bean that I first thought a stone and treated like
one anyway,
chucking them into the awful trash with all those lentils--
ones that were out-of-round
or not properly green or yellow or brown.

Sieving the soup, I understood,
too late, that all were equally good.
The picking and trashing were blunder and waste.
I'd not know now how the real thing should taste.

I thought: what a helluva way to run a soup!

The package should read

"Get rid of the damned sticks and stones.

"Leave the blessed lentils alone."

VI.

PREPARING FOR THE MILLENNIUM

We shall assemble solemn upon mountaintops,
Strolling up in fashion colors yet to be dictated,
A couple parachuting down, taking vows.

Others will use technical prowess,
      parti- colored ropes,
      freeze-dried food,
      and thin condoms
To attain their summits.

Most will travel in sport vehicles;
Millennium parking will be a hassle.

All across America

For one minute following midnight

Billboards will go dark and casinos dim –

Except where this would cause extreme hardship.

Afterwards, expect years of

world-class oil spills,

unprecedented storms,

occasional nuclear displays.

Check your local listings.

A SIRIUS VIEW OF THE WORLD

Living with a screensaver of the departed
mocks news of those elected with strong mandates.

Haven't they learned that even those appointed for life
face a term limit?

Time to number the planet among their constituents.
Time to quit ranting while there is still air to do so.

A sky that kills the canary poor
will fall also on gated retreats.

Only corals love atolls;
they lack other candidates.

BECOMING MORE AND MORE

--YOU KNOW!--

REMOTE

In college days Dad could reach across states to touch me.
Though I dreaded his calls, I grabbed a ringing phone
as a mutt does a sassy squirrel. We all did.
Cranks warned that we'd become slaves to technology.

Our young hang separately, constantly a'twitter,
Too busy communicating to talk, texting too furiously to think.
A phalanx of friends views my cascading words, but do they read?
Selfies, confessions speed across the universe in search of unintelligent
beings.

We know all about easy buttons
but not about hard buttons pressed elsewhere
that bring meals of lotus and games
where killings increase your score and everyone dies a hero.

Apps provide new problems, then solve them in a blaze.
Remotes control us—universally.
Identity is forfeit. You expire many times a year,
learn daily that you are invalid, mismatched.

Luckily, there are chips of the rarest earth
that want to be helping friends.
They know your birthday and shoe size,
and now they'd like to learn everything else.

From watch towers and crossroads,
from drones, satellites and bunkers,
at every intersection and mall
we are monitored by new gods with bad acne.

They observe without comprehending,
record without feeling.
"Under no circumstances listen...unless instructed to."
"Never intervene...until you have to."

My hand-holding device detects a techie last seen
behind a screen larger than life and better defined.
Is he at an actual desk there or
did he ascend into the cloud for midday nutrients?

Is life a game now or virtually real?
Wait! Convince me first that you are not a robot.
Nevermind! No time for that.
'Toothbrush just texted that it has viruses and worms.

This wired helmet helps them learn all about me.
Phones off; the instructor has arrived.
"All of you here will be helping apps design smarter apps.
"Trust us: you are the cogs essential to progress."

Intelligences advance upon us.
Rustling curtains shroud our lives.
No clearance to look behind them--
not nobody, not nohow.

VII.

◇◇◇◇◇◇◇◇◇◇◇◇◇◇◇◇◇◇◇◇◇◇◇◇◇◇◇◇◇◇◇◇◇◇

AN UNDOCUMENTED MAESTRO AND THE MONKS OF A SHORT DARK AGE

Angel Armand DeMondo wore lifts in his shoes, and his blue-black hair he brushed back into a pompadour an inch tall. The naughty gigolo mustache might have been made with the stroke of a fountain pen. For every rehearsal of the Oak Cliff Civic Orchestra, Señor DeMondo wore his double-breasted blue suit and a shirt engineered with a wing collar--the archaic oddness of his wardrobe ennobled by the bantam dignity of our maestro. The man made the clothes.

It was 1952. A few years later, long-playing records in high fidelity would abruptly force the classics into full bloom again. But for the moment, hearing a symphony meant scratching along, in proper sequence, through both sides of three expensive records almost as thick and ridged as checkers. Hit music had driven even light classics from the radio. The instrument to learn was the piano, and the tunes that made you popular were the dances and ballads to which virile, short-haired veterans fathered a baby boom. Classical music was something taught in an overheated parlor, rehearsed in a studio above a paint store, performed in a church basement.

Señor DeMondo wielded his baton in an old storefront uphill from the city dump. The cracked, yellow-washed walls were trimmed with radiator pipes and old newspaper clippings in Spanish--with Señor DeMond shown young and dashing. The greasy display window looked out upon the pounded and sterile clay of a postage stamp playground and, catty-corner, the drugstore with curling Hallmark cards and thumbed-up comic books where I bought rock candy while waiting for my bus home. Señor DeMondo slept and ate behind curtains in back. For conducting rehearsals and managing paraphernalia, he received a stipend from a municipal government that was unusually enlightened--or, perhaps, insouciant.

He referred to the weekly sessions as rehearsals; but since we never performed anywhere, such improvements as we achieved after a first sight-reading were repaid purely by gains in mutual satisfaction--in sonority and the feat of reaching the final release at the same instant. In music, if nowhere else, virtue is its own reward. I attended with my scratchy fiddle because of vague parental fantasies that their sixth-grader might become a towering virtuoso commanding hundreds of dollars for a single performance while garnering matchless satisfaction. As for the others, many of them older than my folks, I'd guess at various mixes of grit, loneliness and hope--as in a loyal poker circle.

Our best instrumentalist was a jolly, soft-haired lady whose obvious bras clutched her like a lover's hands. With such tight skirts and so much lipstick, she must have been European or something even more exotic. Once, in her absence, the drummer asked off-handedly about "our strumpet on trumpet." Nevermind. She made the high notes ring cleanly and rarely missed a Sunday. When she did, Maestro DeMondo quietly removed any music that featured trumpet, because the old bouncer who pooted out rhythmic accents on second trumpet didn't have enough teeth to sustain a melody. And so it was with everyone else from that poor neighborhood of Dallas: all motley, all mongrel; nobody just a regular working dad or cooking mom. The concertmaster was on other days a juggler and magician at birthday parties. A widow with ivory-yellow hair and taped-up clarinet wore every Sunday the same flowered rayon dress, the top buttonhole frayed from tucking in her handkerchief. The cello section consisted of an affable drunkard on pension. To amuse me, he would roll his bow across the cello's back while pretending to bite the neck in concert with the crunching sound. Our drummer had amongst the blotches on his shriveled arm a tattoo that danced the hula.

Maestro DeMondo looked over the group that gathered of a Sunday and, while conversing in a voice accented and gallant, deftly adjusted the musical program--scaling down the difficulty or doubling parts as needed. While we tuned to the piano, he publicly complimented each lady present, then tapped his baton: "Now let us make music together."

The maestro conducted with eyes closed, his left hand beseeching and chiding. At the end of long phrases, he gulped air like a singer. During the afternoon the trumpeter's lipstick moved from her mouth to her right cheek, where she'd rested the mouthpiece. When the old sailor pelted the snare drum, his nostrils flared; called upon to touch the triangle lightly, his eyes glistened. Our widow swayed through solos like a cobra, her pinkies standing out from the clarinet as if from a royal teacup. Strands of the maestro's well-oiled haired lashed his eyes while dye seeped into his collar.

Occasionally, Sunday strollers paused outside the show window. Though what we heard was music, they must have noticed harsh mistakes. Our maestro would quietly call for a popular march or waltz, but usually the audience drifted on before we could begin our offering. Once, only once, a couple troubled to hear us out and to applaud--and received from behind the dingy glass a deep bow from Señor DeMondo.

The pianist had large yellow dentures and bad breath, yet no one departed without the warm benediction of his great hug. Me he hugged and held onto and also tousled the hair on. He said out loud to everybody that it was a positive blessing to have someone so young come and make music with them every week.